BOB,
The Tree who Became a Star

Kindness you'll find !
Suzanne

Written by
Suzanne Lintz Ives

Illustrated by
Chris Francis

Outskirts Press, Inc.
Denver, Colorado

This book is dedicated...

...to my loving family—David and Stacy Lintz and his children, Alex and Kate; Bill and Judy Lintz and their children, Andy and Sarah plus her daughter, Sedona; Ralph and Dot Lintz and their children, Chuck and Ellen, as well as their respective spouses, Carrie Lintz and Sean Dempsey; also to Chuck and Carrie's daughter, Rylie.

...to my mother and father and my dear friend, Don, who are stars in the sky, the ones closest to the moon.

...to my cousins in the Day families, the Elmstrom families, the Fedora families, the Horr families, the Castles families, the Wood families and the Lintz families.

...and to Bob and Harold.

...and to those kind souls already mingling among the twinkling, shining stars, and to those who remember them.

Outskirts Press, Inc.
http://www.outskirtspress.com

ISBN: 978-1-4327-2748-2

Outskirts Press and the "OP" logo are trademarks belonging to Outskirts Press, Inc.

PRINTED IN THE UNITED STATES OF AMERICA

Special acknowledgement...

...to my wonderful and creative Canadian illustrator, Chris Francis, who brought "Bob" to life in pictures.

...to my delightful friend and clever designer, Kitty Nicholason, who magically synchronized text to image and put the lyrics to the music.

...to Marilyn Hunt who asked me to read my story to her 2nd grade class at Chatfield Elementary School in Grand Junction, Colorado.

...to Saundra Hammett who asked me every month for 72 months, "How's the book coming?"

...to Chris Hoffman who inspired the "Boblettes."

...to Brian and Linda Mahoney who offered brilliant comment.

...to Tina Fredericks who caused me to change the story for the better.

...and to the friends and strangers I asked to read and critique my book.

...and finally, the inspiration for "Bob, the Tree who Became a Star," to some anonymous family in Portland, Oregon, who had one of the worst Christmas trees I've ever seen.

This is a story about a little tree
who didn't know what he wanted to be.

A great big oak, all sturdy and tall, or a
tiny little shrub who turned red in the fall.

He was born in a forest that was green and bright,
and he lived there all day and all through the night.

His days were sunny, and he
  had lots of friends.
They'd play on his branches 'til
  his long arms would bend.

In the summer there were picnics,
  and he was the shade.
When the rain started falling,
  it was shelter he made.

Little chirping birds made nests in his boughs,
while under his branches, mooed calves and cows.

The perfume of his pine wafted up to the sky,
and met up with kites way high on the fly.

Around his trunk, pine needles piled high,
and offered sweet cover when others passed by.

"When I grow up, what shall I be?
Shall I stay as I am, a kind little tree?"

What fun they'd have—birds and animals abound.
And then one day, they all looked around.

The summer was over; other trees turned gold.
Our tree in the forest thought he, too, was old.

He thought to himself, and he talked to his friends:
"What will we do when summer really ends?"

They met one night and made wishes on a star.
"We wish to be kind—no matter where we are."

The days wore on, and nights began to chill.
Soon there were children on a nearby hill.

Sleds were sliding on the shining slopes.
And the growing-up tree had grown-up hopes.

"When I'm fully grown, I know what I'll be —
I want to become a Christmas tree."

He shook has branches, and the snow fell down.
Children gasped when they looked around.

"Hey, look at that—it's a beautiful tree!
As beautiful a tree as a tree can be."

They gathered him up and took him to town.
The townsfolk gathered from all around.

He was decked out all over —
    lights shining and bright.
On the very tip-top, an angel held tight.

Such a glorious Christmas
    for all who came.
They adored the tree,
    and they gave him a name.

"Let's call him Harold."
"No, I think he's a Bob."

"But what happens to him
when he's finished his job?"

When presents were opened
and all put away,
The folks turned to Bob and
said, "You can't stay."

"So, what's to become of me?"
he cried.
Some decorated trees had
already died.

Bob remembered that night
in the forest so far
when he and his friends had
pledged on a star.

So the folks—right then—
made a very fine pact...
They'd return Bob to his friends
for his final act.

One morning was perfect—it started to snow.
They put Bob on the van and were ready to go.

They packed up their snacks and their very best sled,
and away they all went to put Bob to bed.

They found a fine spot they thought was just right
and undid the ropes to which Bob snuggled tight.

All Bob's best friends began gathering 'round.
They chimed, "Welcome back" to their friend re-found.

All day they all played in the warmth of the sun,
and each one agreed it was the very best fun.

As the moon began rising, the folks felt a chill.
Then Bob had the idea that gave him a thrill.

"If only my family could be warmed by a fire,
they'd feel the warmth of my love; my heart's desire!

"I know what it means to have family and friends.
I want to be with them 'til their lives end.

"My plan is to join all the stars in the sky,
I'll always shine brightly, and by-and-by...

"Each time they look to the stars above,
they'll see me there and remember my love."

It was at that moment when Bob's dream came true.
The smoke of his branches reached up to the blue.

Suddenly, all beings in the forest bold,
looked up to the sky: Behold! Behold!

Bob starred in the sky ever so bright.
He was winking and smiling and loving the night.

Now, ever after, when you look to the sky,
you'll see Bob shining, a twinkle in his eye.

Bob blinks down a message
for each one to mind:
"You'll always be remembered
if you try to be kind."

But that wasn't all we learned from our Bob,
Love continues to grow, never ending its job...

When a pine tree is cut with branches below,
The limbs on the tree will continue to grow.

And then there were pine cones Bob left on the ground.
From their seeds came "Boblettes" who grew all around.

Bob taught us belonging and being kind
is the very first thing we should keep on our mind.

If you want to be a star, it's easy to do.
Just give love to others and keep some for you.

It's that way with loving and being kind.
Love will prosper and grow, and kindness you'll find!

The End